Kylie Minogue

A Little Golden Book® Biography

AF751753

By Mia Ashley

Illustrated by Caroline Garcia

A GOLDEN BOOK

Penguin Random House Australia is part of the Penguin Random House group
of companies whose addresses can be found at global.penguinrandomhouse.com.
First published by Penguin Books, an imprint of Penguin Random House Australia Pty Ltd, in 2026
Text copyright © Penguin Random House Australia Pty Ltd
Illustrations copyright © Caroline Garcia 2026
Design by Rebecca King © Penguin Random House Australia Pty Ltd
The moral right of the author and illustrator has been asserted.
All rights reserved. No part of this publication may be reproduced, published,
performed in public or communicated to the public in any form or by any means
without prior written permission from Penguin Random House Australia Pty Ltd,
Penguin Random House LLC or its authorised licensees.
Golden Books, A Golden Book, A Little Golden Book, the G colophon,
and the distinctive gold spine are registered trademarks of Penguin Random House LLC.
Printed and bound in China
A catalogue record for this book is available from the National Library of Australia
ISBN 978 1 76 135885 2 (Hardback)

ABBA

Kylie Ann Minogue was born on 28 May 1968 in Melbourne, Australia. She has a younger brother named Benjamin and a younger sister named Dannii.

Growing up, she enjoyed reading and learning to play instruments. She loved music, especially listening to artists such as ABBA and Olivia Newton-John.

While she was sometimes shy around others, Kylie always loved performing. She and Dannii even took singing and dancing lessons. Together, they auditioned for a role in the TV show *The Sullivans*.

The part eventually went to Kylie, but Dannii later got to appear in the show too.

Kylie might not have known it then, but her role on *The Sullivans* marked the beginning of an exciting adventure.

Still only a teenager, she performed a song on the TV program *Young Talent Time* in 1986 with Dannii, who was a show regular.

Australia, and the world, then adored watching Kylie on the TV soap *Neighbours*, after she landed the role of Charlene, the mechanic. The famous wedding episode between her character and Scott, played by Jason Donovan, was watched by two million people in Australia and more than 20 million people in the UK!

Just a week later, Kylie released her debut song, 'The Loco-Motion'.

People everywhere sang along to the catchy tune and fell in love with Kylie's voice! It led to her first record deal with a big music label, Mushroom Records.

With her debut album, *Kylie*, she became Australia's musical girl next door.

Kylie worked hard to create the best music possible, despite critics saying at the time that pop songs all sounded the same.

She switched up the style of her music in 1994 with her song 'Confide in Me'. It topped the charts!

Kylie was growing in confidence as a musician and was also discovering the groovy dance sound for which she would soon become known.

Kylie's world was spinning! In 2000, her smash-hit single 'Spinning Around' proved Kylie had found the sound that resonated with music lovers but also showed her creativity.

Kylie loved to express herself through fashion, too. The gold hot pants she wore in a music video would become so iconic, they were later displayed in the Arts Centre in Melbourne!

Kylie is not afraid to try different styles and is always true to herself.

Globally, Kylie's success was reaching new heights.

In 2001, her album *Fever* and the dance floor hit 'Can't Get You Out of My Head' captured the attention of American fans and she went on to win her first Grammy award for the song 'Come into My World'.

While performing on a world tour, Kylie learned that she had breast cancer. She cancelled the rest of her tour to focus on getting well and was declared cancer-free a year later.

Even when going through tough times, Kylie makes sure to use her platform for good. She supports cancer charities and research to this day.

She is also known as a fierce advocate for the LGBTQ+ community. Kylie's uplifting music and joyous performances bring people together, whatever their differences.

Years later, Kylie is still a big music star! She is the only female artist to have a number one album in five back-to-back decades.

WOW!

She continues to try different types of music, even recording a country-dance album in 2018. No matter the trends or what the industry might expect, she remains true to herself and the music that brings her the most happiness.

Kylie's unique vocals and love of dance inspire generations. Her song 'Padam Padam' earned her a second Grammy award and hundreds of millions of streams. Kylie's 2025 tour received rave reviews from fans of all ages!

Kylie Minogue has remained a pop icon because she's not afraid to break free from people's expectations and try new things. She is the highest-selling Australian female artist of all time.

At the heart of it all, Kylie loves music and sharing that love of music with others. She is treasured by millions of fans because of her kindness, authenticity and talent.